A GUIDE TO EARLY CANADIAN GLASS

a Guide to

EARLY CANADIAN GLASS

HILDA & KELVIN SPENCE

LONGMANS CANADA LIMITED

Longmans Canada Limited
55 Barber Greene Road
Don Mills, Ontario

Printed in Canada
by Hunter Rose Company

Photographs are by the authors.
The articles illustrated are from the
authors' collection except where noted.

CONTENTS

6

7

8 Wﾟ Wᴵᵀᴴ ᴛʜᴇ ꜰɪʀꜱᴛ ᴊᴀɴɢʟᴇ of the old sleigh-bells as the collector opens a dealer's door a bewildering array of glass is seen. Probably some of it is early Canadian, and the problem is to recognize the treasures among the trash. Then, of all times, 'one picture is worth a thousand words.'

This book is intended as a visual guide for the collector of early Canadian glass. Others have done much more research, and a considerable amount of the history of the old glassworks and their products has been given by Gerald Stevens in his books *Early Canadian Glass* and *In a Canadian Attic*. The purpose here is to show in photographs what has already been learned, so that the collector may not only take with him on his explorations pictures of what to look for, but may have a starting-point from which to push on to new discoveries.

Pity the collector of old silver; he misses all the fun of being a detective! When he turns over an old spoon the identification is right there, stamped into it — the country of origin, the maker's initials, and an indication of the date. Nothing of that kind appears on old glass, or at least on old Canadian glass. One must start in with the deductive process, looking for clues in its shape, size, pattern, colour and quality that may relate it directly or indirectly to some shard that has been dug out of the ground at the site of an old glassworks, some piece that has been reliably identified by persons with a knowledge of its history or source, or some piece illustrated in an old glass-company catalogue.

The beginner nowadays starts with the advantage that this work of identification has already been done on a number of designs and patterns, some of which are not too difficult to find and acquire as an authentic nucleus of a collection. He may then start working from the known to the unknown, using such clues or bits of evidence, or processes of deduction or logic, as may develop.

Comparing shapes and sizes often gives a lead. For example, the distinctive rounding of the foot of the 'Maple Leaf' comport is found on several other established Canadian patterns and not on any known American pattern.

Thus if one should come across an article with still a different, unknown pattern, but with that typical size and shape of foot, it would be wise to buy it before the price goes up!

Comparing colours of clear glass is seldom a reliable test. The bluish or greenish tinge of glass made from natural sand may vary from one batch to another in the same glassworks, and moreover two or more producers may have got their sand from the same source, as did the St. Johns and Como-Hudson companies of Quebec. As an experiment the authors once searched through their boxes of raw glass, all dug up at the site of one of the old Como factories, and laid in a row a progression of fragments, each varying only slightly in colour from the last, that ran from the deepest brown through amber to bluish to greenish to clear, uncoloured glass.

In figured pressed glass, comparing patterns is obviously a useful guide. Occasionally it leads to surprising results, because of the habit of some of the old glass-makers of mixing up their patterns by taking a bit of one and working it into another. Thus you will sometimes find an example of an unidentified pattern that contains a figure or medallion from one that is well known and fully authenticated. Suddenly you are upon a peak in Darien!

The old moulds sometimes had small defects that showed up in piece after piece that they produced. We were once able to identify one of our treasures positively as a duplicate of one in the museum, because a small chip in the edge of the mould had left the same little extra gob of glass on both pieces.

In the old glassworks the moulds were fashioned by hand and cast right in the mould-room of the plant, and a mould made in another plant, even if intended as a copy, was never exactly the same. The four Hudson hand-lamps pictured in this book, three coloured and one of clear ribbed glass, all have rayed bottoms. Some of the rays are slightly narrower than others, but there is no regularity in the location of these narrow rays around the circle; yet in each lamp they appear in the same positions. Other lamps are superficially the same, but when the rays are examined they are found to have come from different moulds.

In pattern glass particularly, the negative approach is most important. You should know what *not* to buy at least as well as what to seek. Buy or borrow books on American glass such as those by Ruth Webb Lee and Alice Hulett Metz, and pore over them until you have a good familiarity with American patterns. Then, before you decide that you have discovered a new Canadian pattern, go back and consult Lee and Metz again. Despite everything, you will get caught once in a while — at least *we* still do.

This is not to say that there is no Canadian glass in the Lee or Metz books. There is. Unfortunately many of the finest products of the old Canadian craftsmen, including their glass, have for years been bought up and moved across the border, there to be sold as 'early American.' So if you have some good reason for suspecting your pattern to be Canadian do not give up merely because you find it in Lee or Metz; check first to see whether they show an established American origin.

The fact that an article is found in some numbers in one area and not elsewhere may give a clue to its origin. There is a certain plain goblet plentiful all around St. Johns, Quebec, and through the Eastern Townships, but less frequently found elsewhere. On a larger scale, some patterns are well known from coast to coast in Canada, but found only rarely in the United States.

Then, of course, there are the pieces that are so crude or so vastly hideous that one cannot imagine anyone going to the trouble of importing them. Don't be too sure, however, for our Victorian ancestors must have imported that appalling 'Carnival' glass by the ton; heaven forbid that anyone discover it was made here!

Practically none of the known Canadian glass is what is properly called flint glass; it is made without lead, and has very little ring when tapped. In fact if a piece is found to have the clear musical ring of flint glass this is a cause for doubting its Canadian origin, although some of the old advertisements indicated that special orders would be made with lead if required.

There is a common misconception that the age of pressed glass can be judged by the number of pieces in the mould. In fact whether a specimen is made from a two-piece, three-piece or four-piece mould is of no significance. The number of moulds usually varied with the complexity of the pattern.

Much is said in this book about Ontario, Quebec and the Maritimes, but let it not be thought that the hunting-grounds are limited to these regions. We have found old Canadian glass, including some rare pieces, in almost every western city from Winnipeg to Victoria, carried there no doubt in the belongings of those easterners who settled in the West fifty years or more ago.

The search is only beginning, and there are still clues to be dug out of the ground and treasures to be discovered in out-of-the-way places. There are old records to be searched and old factory sites to be located. Dozens of patterns that no one has yet identified are found in numbers on Canadian dealers' shelves but seldom south of the border. Today they can be had for next to nothing; tomorrow some of them may be treasures.

Happy sleuthing!

HILDA AND KELVIN SPENCE

II

"Cavagnal"
Como, Quebec
July, 1966

Chapter One

THE FRENCH RÉGIME

THE MARQUIS DE DENONVILLE, Governor of New France, to the Minister of State of France, November 13, 1685:

It is not impossible that one could establish a glassworks in this country; the greatest problem is labour, which makes everything so expensive.

Memorandum of Sieur de Catalogne to the Ministry, November 7, 1712:

It is to be hoped that His Majesty will see fit to send to this country all sorts of artisans, especially potters and a glass-blower, *and they will find much to keep them busy.*

We know that the potters were sent very promptly, and the eager generosity with which Louis XIV, and after him the Regency, responded to appeals of this kind from the infant colony strongly suggests that a glass-blower must also have been dispatched. Ships plied back and forth each summer bringing immigrants to Quebec. It is significant, as will appear later, that these ships sailed from the two French ports of La Rochelle and Dieppe.

Soon after Catalogne's plea artisans of various skills began to appear in the colony — experts in the mining and smelting of iron to develop the deposits at St. Maurice, technicians in copper and lead, and above all, specialists in the various crafts related to the building trade. The Government of France was keen to promote the expansion of the colony and to provide dwellings and their amenities for the growing population. It sent out brick-makers, tile-makers, potters and weavers, and although positive records have not yet been found it would have been strange if one of the most sought-after and necessary artisans, the glass-blower to make windows, bottles and such necessities, had been omitted.

Pictured here from the authors' collection are five medicine vials that were in use in the colony during the French Régime. They belonged to the Jesuits, were used by the 'apothecary' priests for dispensing remedies, and were given to the General Hospital of Quebec along with a number of faience jars full of medicines when the Jesuits were winding up their activities and preparing to depart after the Conquest. Dr. Marius Barbeau lists them in his book *Trésor des Anciens Jésuites* as having been received by the hospital in 1787.

Either these vials came from France or they were made in the colony, as the colonists were prohibited from trading elsewhere. Yet the crude, almost amateurish workmanship and design are far removed from the fine, precise and beautifully executed products of the French glass-houses of that period.

The vials are free-blown to extreme thinness, and a spread and involuted base has been formed by pushing the pontil rod into the bottle. Owing to the thinness of the glass the pontil rod has left a hole, which in turn has been crudely sealed over from the inside with a heavy glass cap. Sizes are completely at random and there is no uniformity of shape; heights range from eight inches to $9\frac{1}{4}$, and capacities from just under three ounces to just over six. The glass is made from natural sand which has given it a pale green tinge, and it is full of striations, irregularities and bubbles. One gets the impression that the craftsman was a novice with some knowledge of glass-blowing but little practical skill.

Let it be said at once that identical bottles are occasionally to be found today in France. Where? In local museums and collections *in La Rochelle and far to the north in the little coastal towns near Dieppe.*

Is it only a coincidence that the vials turn up around the only two French ports that had regular contact with the New World? Are we to assume that there were glassworks in these two widely separated spots turning out identical crude products? If so, why were they so different from the products of other contemporary French glass-houses? Or must we believe, on the other hand, that the bottles were made at some central point in France and sent to La Rochelle and Dieppe, whence they reached the New World? And if so, why the irregular shapes and sizes; why such fragile glass to withstand the rigours of shipment in bulk and a month or two on the North Atlantic? The conclusion can hardly be avoided that in New France itself some glass-blower was at work, perhaps an apprentice from a French factory, with little experience and certainly without the tools and facilities available in his homeland, and that some of his bottles held the medicines for the sailors on the long voyage back to France.

Possibly there is a list somewhere in the archives of Ottawa, Quebec or France of the names and occupations of immigrants during the French

Régime; if so it has not yet been searched for the glass-blower so especially requested by Sieur de Catalogne. Meanwhile the evidence indicates that some none too skilful artisan did arrive and ply his craft, and that these vials of his workmanship are specimens of the first Canadian glass.

But there is one other tantalizing possibility that may lead us off into flights of fancy, yet clamours to be recognized. Did the Jesuits themselves, who met necessity resourcefully in so many other ways, try their own hands at glass-blowing even before the time of Sieur de Catalogne?

In 1941 archaeologists from the Royal Ontario Museum commenced excavations at the site of the missionary fort Ste. Marie I, which the Jesuits built in 1639 (near where Midland, Ontario, now stands) and destroyed and abandoned ten years later. (See Kenneth E. Kidd's *The Excavation of Ste. Marie I*, University of Toronto Press, 1949.) Fifty-four fragments of broken glass were turned up; and some of them, when pieced together, produced a bottle about 9½ inches tall and five inches in diameter, with a slender neck, an oval or tear-shaped body and a concave bottom. The glass was extremely thin, pale green, with striations, irregularities and bubbles. The discoverers believed that it must be Venetian, and marvelled at how such a fragile vessel could have survived the dangers of an ocean voyage and the journey up the St. Lawrence and Ottawa Rivers and across the wilderness of forests and rivers to Fort Ste. Marie.

Fragments of another very similar bottle were also found, as well as miscellaneous shards of pale green and of colourless glass.

It is perhaps not unreasonable to suggest that if any amateur were to experiment with glass-blowing, say with melted-down fragments of broken window-panes, the object he would be most likely to produce would be a thin-walled, tear-shaped vessel with striations and bubbles and a pushed-in bottom to make it stand upright. Yet in all the seventy-three volumes of the *Jesuit Relations* there is no record of attempts at glass-blowing. Window glass itself was a rare commodity, and the *Relations* tell of trade even in cracked or damaged panes, showing how highly it was valued. And window glass in those days had a pale-green colour. . . .

Under British rule manufacturing was at first discouraged; the colony was regarded as an exclusive market for English goods and a source of furs and lumber, and it was not until 1794 that under Jay's Treaty the colonists secured the right of reciprocal trade with the United States. Thereafter articles of glass could be imported, subject to duty, from south of the border, and no doubt some of the very old free-blown pieces that are occasionally found in Canada entered this country from the United States in the early part of the nineteenth century.

However, ordinary glass is not difficult to make wherever good sand and a source of fuel are available, whereas its products are not easy to transport for long distances. Windows and bottles are in demand wherever there are habitations. These considerations would lead one to expect that small local glassworks might have been established here and there as the colony grew, making such things as the crude window-pane pictured in our final chapter. In fact one such plant is believed to have been operating at Mallorytown, Ontario about 1825, and Gerald Stevens has also pointed to the possibility that a glassworks may have been established in Cayuga, county of Haldimand, in 1836.

Perhaps in time more sites of this kind will be discovered, especially in the Maritimes where the need for local production was greater because the seaboard colonies had no land routes at the time for trading with the United States under Jay's Treaty, and were prohibited by the Navigation Laws from trading by sea. The Navigation Laws were not repealed until 1849.

While, as stated, glass as a material was not difficult to make, the fabrication of it into window-panes, bottles or table-ware for commercial purposes required a considerable degree of experience and skill. Thus, for example, although there are no known records of what the Mallorytown enterprise produced, we are bound to assume that its glass-blowers came from some of the nearby American factories and produced the same free-blown products that they had made in the United States. This makes it impossible to identify any glass as being from a small early plant such as Mallorytown unless the history of the individual piece is known, and the likelihood of finding an example such as those in the Royal Ontario Museum, whose history can be followed back with any certainty for 140 years, is exceedingly remote.

As the century progressed and the colony developed in population, transportation and self-reliance, business expanded beyond the local suppliers into partnerships and companies serving a larger field, and in Lower Canada the first organized production of glass for the Canadian market had its beginnings. The Quebec houses were to dominate that market for the next thirty years.

THERE SHOULD BE, in justice, a chapter in this book devoted solely to the products of the first of the large glass companies to appear on the Canadian scene, which under various names and reorganizations has continued to this day. Unfortunately that is not possible, because so very few of its earlier products have yet been traced. The glassworks at St. Johns, Quebec, went into production with two furnaces in the spring of 1845, drawing sand from Beauharnois and Vaudreuil and turning out one hundred half-boxes of window glass a day. Soon the plant was also producing table-ware, at first free-blown such as the two earlier goblets pictured here, and later in various designs of moulded and pattern glass of which we have little record. There is a fruitful field here for research among the unidentified designs and patterns that keep turning up around St. Johns and the Eastern Townships.

The original name of the St. Johns company is unknown, but by 1855 it had become Foster Brothers. About 1879 the name was changed to Excelsior Glass Company and shortly afterwards the plant was moved to Montreal and continued under other names as described in the next chapter.

The beginnings at St. Johns were closely followed by a glass company at what is now the village of Como, in the county of Vaudreuil. This was organized under the name of Masson and Company in 1845 and went into production in 1846 or 1847. It was reorganized as Ottawa Glass Company in 1847 but was dissolved in December 1848. The glass-blowers who thus lost employment obtained financial help from Montreal and at once organized a new company, Canada Glass Works, which built a new plant in Como and later bought the old one, operating both from 1850 on.

About 1855 another company, which was apparently quite independent of these and known as British-American Glass Company, set up a plant about a mile away in the village of Hudson. It changed its name later to Montreal Glass Company and by 1867 was known as Canada Glass Company, having apparently absorbed or been absorbed by its Como competitors. In 1871 it was incorporated as a limited company with the name Canada Glass Works Company Limited. The Como-Hudson operations ceased in 1875.

These Como-Hudson companies turned out quantities of purely utilitarian window glass and druggists' and soft-drink bottles, but they also produced blown and moulded articles of various kinds in colours of amber, deep blue, clear and semi-opaque pale blue, green, and magenta, some of which are of considerable artistic merit. Neither shards, records nor authenticated specimens have yet given any reliable indication that pattern glass was made in the Como-Hudson plants.

Two other glass-houses lived and died during this period: John C. Spence of Montreal, who specialized in glass staining in the eighteen-fifties and sixties, and St. Lawrence Glass Company, which operated a large factory in Montreal for the production of all kinds of glassware between 1867 and 1875. Few of the Spence products and none of the St. Lawrence products have been authenticated, and here again work is beckoning the amateur sleuth.

The period from 1845 to 1875 belonged to Quebec. True, there was some production after 1857 in New Brunswick, and in 1865 the first Hamilton company was having its beginnings, but nearly all of the Canadian glass that today we may properly call antique, as being over one hundred years old, was made in these large Quebec glass-houses.

PLATE 2 *The mould-blown bowl of this lamp is clear, colourless non-lead glass in which are embedded vertical, slightly swirled stripes of light-blue opal glass which run together at top and bottom. It has been attached to a clear pressed-glass base. The bowl is ribbed as well as striped, the ribbing being on the inside as in the Hudson lamp in Plate 9. Another example of these pale-blue stripes is found in the whimsy or witch-ball pictured in Plate 5, blown by James Stevenson of Hudson. The opal glass, of which quantities are found on the site of the Hudson factory, is a somewhat paler blue than was made in later times, and the striping, ribbing, colour and technique are all characteristic of products of the Canada Glass Co., Hudson, and its successor from 1871 to 1875, Canada Glass Works Co. Ltd. The chimney, while of an early pattern, cannot be definitely identified.*

PLATE 3 *Four goblets from St. Johns, Que., showing the progress of the art of glass-making in that factory. From the left: (1) very heavy crudely fashioned free-blown goblet; (2) free-blown goblet but of improved design and thinner glass, lightly etched by sand or acid; (3) pressed-glass goblet, plain; (4) highly tailored pressed-glass goblet, decorated on a wheel.*

PLATE 4 *'Beaver' goblet, Excelsior Glass Co., St. Johns, Que., 1880. The beaver-and-maple-leaf decoration is well executed, and inscribed on the under side of the foot in raised letters are the words 'St. Jean Baptiste. Quebec. 24 Juin 1880.'*

Clearly this was made for a special day and purpose, and probably for that reason not many were produced. In any event examples are now very rare.

24 PLATE 5 *Three fully authenticated whimsies, products of the Como-Hudson glassworks: a delicately executed pale-green chain drape, property of Mr. R. A. Blenkinship of Hudson; a witch-ball of clear glass with embedded stripes of pale-blue opal glass owned by Miss Irene Lancaster of Como; and a large magenta-coloured witch-ball belonging to Mrs. Enid Darrell of Choisy, Que. Miss Lancaster and Mrs. Darrell are descendants of James Stevenson, the glass-blower who made both witch-balls.*

PLATE 6 *Four prescription bottles of greenish bottle-glass that were in use between 1845 and 1855, when only St. Johns and Como-Hudson are known to have been operating, and therefore assumed to be of Quebec origin. The one on the left is a chloroform bottle from the original drugstore of J. D. B. Fraser of Pictou, N.S., who was noted as the first person in Canada to use anaesthetic, having administered it to his wife in childbirth in 1847. The second bottle, probably an early product of St. Johns, is even more crudely made. The third and fourth contained respectively Dr. Stafford's and Dr. Beach's 'Vegetable Compositions,'*

prepared by C. S. Harris of Manchester, Canada West, and some in the authors' possession are still filled, labelled and wrapped. Manchester, C.W. existed under that name only from 1850 to 1856.

PLATE 7 *Pickle bottle, height eight inches, diameter 2⅞ inches, greenish bottle-glass, heavily clouded and slightly iridescent from long exposure, found in the earth under a very old building on the site of the second Como factory. A number of shards from the site identify this as a product of Canada Glass Works, c. 1849.*

28

PLATE 8 *This beautifully shaped decorative bottle was handed down through the family of one of the owners of the Canada Glass Works, Hudson, and is now owned by Dunbar Mullan of Hudson. It is almost transparent blue glass in the middle, tapering to pale opaque blue at the top and bottom. It is free-blown, with a pontil mark on the base.*

PLATE 9 *This type of ribbed and swirled lamp with applied handle was authenticated some years ago by Gerald Stevens as a product of the Como-Hudson glassworks. Further reference is made to this lamp in the introduction and the notes to Plate 14.*

30

PLATE 10 *Pair of witch-balls of greenish bottle-glass; whimsies blown by Amédé Ladurantais at one of the Como-Hudson plants* C. *1870.*

32 PLATE 11 *Shards excavated at the Como and Hudson sites confirm that bottles identical to these in shape and in the dark-blue and lighter-blue colours were made in these factories. The larger bottle is the same size and shape as the Campbell's Elixir bottle, Plate 13.*

PLATES 12 AND 13 *Two bottles, one five inches high, the other thirteen inches. The smaller is embossed with the words 'Campbell & Co., Medical Hall, Montreal'; the other bears the name on the label, 'Kenneth Campbell & Co.'; both are of greenish bottle-glass. Kenneth Campbell & Co. were important wholesale druggists at 677 Craig Street, Montreal, with a retail branch in Medical Hall, which was in Morgan's block, Phillips Square. The company was established in 1856, and continued for some years thereafter. With both St. Johns and Como-Hudson manufacturing druggists' bottles it seems inevitable that one or both must have supplied this large drug firm.*

PLATE 14 *Three coloured-glass hand-lamps,*
c. 1870, of the Canada Glass Co., Hudson,
all blown into the same mould as the clear
ribbed and swirled lamp in Plate 9. This
was possible because the swirled ribbing
of the clear-glass lamp was on the inside,
just as the blue-striped lamp (Plate 2) is
ribbed inside with a smooth exterior. It

*would be interesting to know how this was
accomplished; apparently it was a special
technique much used by the Como-Hudson
glass-blowers. Note that all of the lamps
have applied handles; those with moulded
handles are of a later period and uncertain
origin.*

Chapter Four

THE LATE NINETEENTH CENTURY AND BEYOND

A GLANCE at the diagram on page 108 will show that as all but one of the Quebec houses succumbed to the pressure of United States competition, new companies were in the ascendant in Ontario and the Maritimes. The emphasis during this period was on figured pressed glass, or pattern glass, which was produced in ever increasing quantities. Some of the patterns were fully a match in taste and execution for anything of the kind made in other countries, but eventually, perhaps about the turn of the century, amalgamations and the drive for greater volume seem to have caused a deterioration in the quality of design and craftsmanship. With some notable exceptions the glass began to *look* machine-made even before it was.

Once more, the patterns we know are only a few of those that were produced. Probably there were also other glass-houses whose names have been forgotten. The census of 1891 shows twelve glassworks in Canada; we know of only seven.

The Hamilton Glass Works began in 1865, but apparently produced little but bottles and druggists' ware, and it was not until 1875 that the Burlington Glass Company opened its plant in Hamilton. Almost from the start its output of all kinds of glassware was substantial. Much research has been done on this company and many of its products are identified.

In 1881 the first of the Nova Scotia plants opened, followed nine years later by two others, and a number of their patterns also have become well known, although sometimes puzzling, to the collector. The puzzle comes from the fact that a pattern well established as originating in one house will be found mixed with a pattern from another, although the two houses were in competition. These peculiar hybrids are found in large numbers.

In between these two sources, Ontario and the Maritimes, there is a baffling gap in our knowledge of the last quarter of the century — Quebec. The St. Lawrence Glass Company, Montreal, 1867-75, had a large, impressive factory and turned out all kinds of glassware, of which we have no authenticated specimen whatever. The Excelsior Glass Company of St. Johns was moved to a new plant in Montreal in 1881, and produced bottles and pressed glassware, of which we have very little knowledge. In 1885 it became the

North American Glass Company, and in 1892 the Diamond Glass Company, becoming eventually the Dominion Glass Company that we know today.

A hint from George MacLaren's brochure *Nova Scotia Glass* may give us a clue to part of the Quebec problem. He mentions that in 1892 the Nova Scotia Glass Company, which had been bought out by the Diamond Glass Company, was closed 'and the moulds were sent to Montreal.' Similarly the Lamont Glass Company was absorbed by the Diamond Company in 1897, and closed in 1899. No doubt the Lamont moulds were also sent to Montreal.

It seems probable that the quantities of the 'Starflower' pattern, and of the 'Prism and Diamond' and its variants, still found through Quebec, were made by the Diamond Company from the moulds of the Nova Scotia Glass Company, and that when the Lamont 'Pillar' moulds were also acquired the Diamond Company interchanged patterns, so that we find a 'Pillar' base on a 'Prism and Diamond' bowl with a 'Starflower' finial on the cover. It may also explain the small nappies long credited to the Nova Scotia Company but appearing in great numbers in Quebec and Ontario, and the low comports of identical design found in Quebec both in plain and in coloured glass (Plates 39-42).

When did the era of 'early glass' end? 'Early Canadian' is an inexact term, and one can only say that the period drew to a close when the quickening pace of life and the desire for bigger companies, higher profits and higher wages forced mass production into this as into so many other industries. Perhaps, too, the rigours of the first Great War left the public less demanding and more tolerant of machine-made goods. In any event, after the first ten or fifteen years of the twentieth century the craftsmen of the Victorian age dwindled away and slowly disappeared. These skilful artisans with their handle-bar moustaches, their galluses, their whimsies and parades and their incomparable deftness of hand finally yielded to the economy of the machine.

PLATE 15 *Two small hand-lamps, one in blue bearing the lettering on the outside 'l'Ange Gardien—Extra—C. H. Binks and Co. Montreal,' and the other plain, in green. Gerald Stevens has done a great deal of research on the 'Guardian Angel' lamps, which were used not only in private houses but in churches and religious ceremonials in Quebec, and he has learned that Binks and Co. operated in Montreal as importers from 1877 to 1905. The surprising thing is that although Binks and the church-supply houses were within a few blocks of the Montreal office and warehouse of the Excelsior Glass Co. (whose plant at St. Johns, incidentally, was near the village of l'Ange Gardien), Mr. Stevens has found from excavation of shards that at least some clear-glass lamps bearing this lettering were made in Hamilton, Ont.*

The 'Guardian Angel' lamps come in various colours and clear glass; they are of different small sizes and shapes and some are even more 'bilingual' than the one pictured, having 'Guardian Angel' printed in both French and English. All have applied handles, some finished at the bottom with a flourish or 'trail,' and all are exceedingly rare. A remarkable example we have seen has the handle applied on the wrong side so that it covers part of the lettering. The globes or shades and the metal fittings are interchangeable and cannot be identified.

The other lamp in the picture is so precisely identical in every measurement, even when gauged with calipers, that one would say it must have come from the same mould were it not that the 'Angel' mould bore lettering. However there is one difference between the two: whereas the 'Angel' lamp shows the distinct marks of the two-piece mould into which the glass was blown, the plain lamp has been turned in the mould so that no mould-marks show. Can it be that this was done to eradicate the lettering as well as the mould-marks? This conjecture is encouraged by the fact that there are very faint lines or scorings around the bowl just where the printing would have been.

PLATE 16 *The pattern, known as 'Filly,' of the spoon-holder on the left has been attributed by Gerald Stevens to the Burlington Glass Co., a butter dish of that pattern, said to have been made in the Burlington Works, having been acquired* *in Hamilton. The 'Pointed Bull's-eye' pattern on the right is stated by the same authority to have been produced in many Canadian glass-houses.*

PLATE 17 *'Beaded Grape' bowl. Examples of this pattern are said to have been made by the Burlington Glass Co. of Hamilton. It was also produced in large quantities in the U.S., in both clear and green glass. Be cautious with this pattern, as there are strong indications that modern reproductions of it are on the market. The original examples in the green glass had gold on the beading which is said to be omitted in the reproductions. This is not a test for the clear glass, where one can judge only by the appearance and feel of the glass.*

PLATE 18 *For a long time the pattern
of this butter dish was a puzzle. It is
clearly 'Starflower,' but whereas in the
well-known Nova Scotia 'Starflower' the
sprig bearing the flowers is intertwined
with leaves of a different plant, perhaps
lily-of-the-valley, here the two plants are
separated. Moreover, this pattern places
more emphasis upon the 'dewdrops,' the
glass is of greater brilliance, and the knob or
handle is of a shape not encountered in
Nova Scotia 'Starflower.'*

    *The mystery was solved in 1965 when
Gerald Stevens, in excavating at the site
of the New Brunswick Crystal Glass Co.'s
works in East Saint John, N.B., found
shards of this dish, including a handle
of the shape pictured. This is the first
break-through into the products of New
Brunswick. These products pre-date the
Nova Scotia 'Starflower,' for the New
Brunswick Crystal Glass Co. operated only
between 1872 and 1878.*

PLATE 19 *Nova Scotia 'Starflower' covered sugar bowl. This pattern is found from coast to coast in Canada in every form, from nappies to goblets and large covered comports. Whole convents have been stocked with it in Quebec. The pattern almost certainly originated with the* Nova Scotia Glass Co., Trenton, N.S., *copied in part from the earlier New Brunswick pattern, but the moulds were later transferred to Montreal where the Diamond Glass Co. apparently continued to produce the pattern.*

PLATE 20 *Nova Scotia 'Starflower' comport; another example of the pattern described above. Note the similarity of the foot to that of the 'Tassel and Crest' comport, Plate 25.*

PLATE 21 *Comport, butter dish and milk pitcher of the 'Grape and Vine' pattern; probably Nova Scotia Glass Co. about 1886-90. This is one of the best-executed and most attractive patterns in early Canadian glass. The grape-vine is gracefully designed and strongly indicated, and the*

ribbing is done with great precision and definition. This ribbing is clearly distinguishable from ribbing on U.S. glass. The comports come in at least two sizes. Incidentally, the one pictured here had been purchased by a U.S. dealer; one of the writers trailed him into the State of Maine, rescued the comport and had to pay duty to bring it back to Canada! This pattern (in goblets) is referred to in U.S. books as 'Ramsay Grape' but they have no information about it.

PLATE 22 *'Grape and Vine' eleven-inch*
plate. The grid-work or waffle in the centre
is a notable characteristic of several pieces
of this pattern, cleverly designed to catch
the light and add sparkle to the glass.

PLATES 23 AND 24 *Small fruit dish, celery vase and tall comport, attributed to Nova Scotia Glass Co., c. 1886. The name of this pattern is unknown, but it is unmistakably related to the 'Grape and Vine.' From the shape of the foot it might be called 'Corinthian.' The grace of the* design and the superb workmanship shown in the production of this pattern are notable demonstrations of the skill achieved by Canadian artisans of the period.

50 PLATE 25 *'Tassel and Crest' comport.
For some years this pattern has been
attributed to the Humphreys Glass Co.,
Trenton, N.S.; yet the investigation
described by George MacLaren, Curator
of History of the Nova Scotia Museum
(Nova Scotia Glass, 1965) indicates that
the products of the Humphreys Co. were
confined to bottles, lamps and lamp
chimneys, fruit jars, and other articles
of plain, undecorated glass. While the
company undoubtedly employed highly
skilled artisans, as witness a fully authenticated and beautifully wrought cane in our
collection made by one of the Humphreys
glass-blowers, no real evidence has yet
come to light that the company ever
produced commercially any highly
sophisticated pattern glass such as the
'Tassel and Crest.' Even as late as 1906
the productive parts of the large plant
were described as 'bottle shops and
chimney shops.'*

*On the other hand there is every indica-
tion that this pattern originated in Nova
Scotia; that is where most examples are
found today, and it seems to be completely
unknown in the U.S. No one has yet
explained the significance of the 'Crest'
of crossed trumpets, shield, wings and
overhead star, or of the palm trees.
Occasionally one finds a variant of the
'Tassel and Crest' pattern containing
the medallion or shield of the 'Raspberry
and Shield' pattern (Plate 26).*

*The Nova Scotia Glass Co. was established
at Trenton, N.S. in 1881 to make 'all kinds
of glassware.' It was making tableware*

*in 1882, and by 1886-7, with improved
materials and equipment, it was turning
out ware that was 'new and beautifully
designed,' and 'pressed glass, and tumblers
engraved with Masonic and Oddfellow
emblems.' (George MacLaren, op. cit.)*

*Mr. MacLaren has found shards of the
'Raspberry and Shield' at the site of the
factories. With an identical part of that
pattern appearing in the 'Tassel and Crest,'
there is an inference that the same company
made both. The trouble is that all three
factories were on approximately the same
site. If we eliminate Humphreys for the
reasons above, it is practically a toss-up
between the other two, but because of the
resemblance of the crest to the 'Masonic
and Oddfellow emblems' mentioned above
our vote goes to Nova Scotia Glass Co. with
a date about 1887.*

PLATE 26 '*Raspberry*' *plate and*
'*Raspberry and Shield*' *jam jar and cream*
jug, made in Trenton, N.S., c. 1887
probably by Nova Scotia Glass Co. See
notes to Plates 25 and 34. The '*Shield*' *is*
sometimes worked into the '*Tassel and*
Crest' *pattern.*

PLATE 27 'Tassel and Crest' table set. This pattern was one of the first to become known as Canadian, and it is now found only rarely in the shops. In addition to the objects pictured here, there are large and small nappies or fruit dishes and covered comports of seven-inch and eight-inch diameter. As to the origin and date of this pattern see notes to Plate 25.

PLATE 28 *Queen Victoria Golden Jubilee plate and covered bowl. While it has been said that this pattern was produced in many Canadian glass-houses, we do not know of any proof that it was made by others besides the Nova Scotia Glass Co., c. 1887. The decoration is typical of that house; for example, compare the sprays of leaves and berries with those on the skirt of the 'Grape and Vine' comport and pitcher, Plate 21. There are variations of this plate, one with the Queen's picture turned ninety degrees and surrounded by a sunburst instead of the wreath, and another*

with two pictures of the Queen, one as at the time of her coronation in 1837, and the other, superimposed, as in 1887. The covered bowl is exceedingly rare, the plate somewhat rare.

PLATE 29 *'Pillar' open comport. This is perhaps the handsomest of all the Canadian patterns. Research by Ian Morgan of Montreal has confirmed that it was made by Lamont Glass Co., Trenton, N.S., 1890-1902. The glass is heavy and clear, and the design and workmanship are excellent. Comports, both open and covered, come in several sizes.*

PLATE 30 *A complete table set of spoon-holder, cream jug, sugar bowl and butter dish in the Lamont 'Pillar' pattern.*

PLATE 31 *Covered cheese dish, another fine
example of the Lamont 'Pillar' pattern.
The decoration of the dish itself is
exceptionally striking, and is deeply impressed
and very smoothly finished.*

PLATE 32 *Egg-cups, height 4½″, width across top 2⅜″, across foot 2¾″. Many Canadian glass-houses must have turned out pressed-glass egg-cups, as numbers of them are to be found. The ones pictured are authenticated specimens from the Humphreys Co., Trenton, N.S., and the bowls are curved slightly inward at the top, which may be a distinguishing feature.*

58

PLATE 33 *Tumbler, very thin clear glass, etched with Lord's Prayer, said to have been made by Lamont Glass Co. in the 1890's. This is an unusual item; the only other specimen known to us is in the Royal Ontario Museum.*

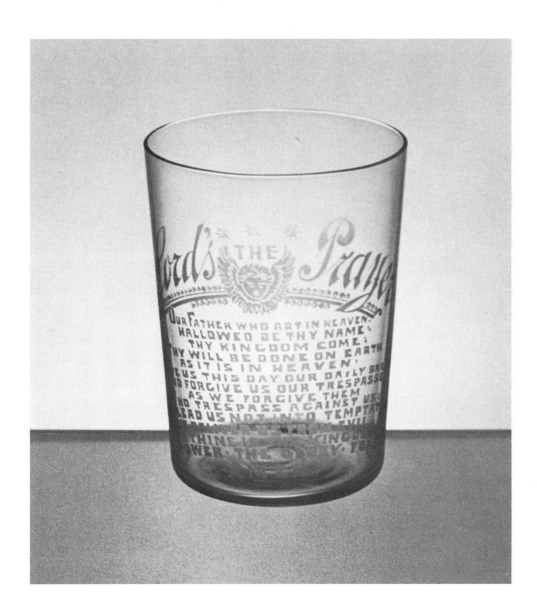

PLATE 34 *Five Nova Scotian goblets; from left to right, (1) 'Raspberry and Shield,' (2) 'Gothic,' (3) 'Pillar,' (4) 'Tandem Bicycle,' and (5) 'Kenlee.' The 'Raspberry' is a very curious pattern in several respects; sometimes it carries the shield or medallion, sometimes not, and the same medallion is occasionally found as a variant in the 'Tassel and Crest' pattern. Also, although there is no doubt of the Nova Scotian origin of this glass, the 'Raspberry' part of the pattern turns up in identical form in the U.S. 'Egyptian' pattern. Who borrowed from whom?*

The 'Gothic' and 'Pillar' are claimed in the U.S. books to be early American, but this is only because examples have been carried across the border; they definitely belong to Canada. A party from the Nova Scotia Museum excavating at the Trenton, N.S. site in 1964 found shards of 'Raspberry and Shield,' 'Gothic' and 'Kenlee.' 'Tandem Bicycle' still lacks the positive proof of origin possessed by the others, but it is a near relative of 'Gothic' and there is little doubt that as the site is further explored shards of the 'Tandem Bicycle' pattern will be uncovered.

PLATE 35 *Four more goblets, at least three of them Nova Scotian; left to right, (1) 'Prism and Diamond,' (2) 'Starflower,' (3) 'Grape and Vine,' and (4) 'Ribbed' patterns. All of these patterns are found in various forms of glassware. The first two were probably also made later in Montreal; the first may have originated there. Nos. 3 and 4 are related; one often finds two plates, comports or other pieces that are identical in every respect except that one includes the grape-and-vine decoration, the other bears only the ribbing.*

PLATE 36 *Four nappies, all closely related by similarities of pattern. The third from left is the same as one in the Royal Ontario Museum, identified as 'Dominion Diamond,' Nova Scotia, but this name seems doubtful. The Nova Scotia Glass Co. and the Lamont Glass Co. were bought out and closed by the Diamond Glass Co. of Montreal, but they both appear to have retained their own names to the end, and no company named 'Dominion' was involved. The pattern seems to be Nova Scotian and we believe it is Lamont. The other nappies are variations on the same theme. All four are found in some numbers throughout eastern Canada, and may have been repeated by the Diamond Co. in Montreal after the purchase.*

PLATE 37 *Five miscellaneous Canadian nappies; from left to right, (1) 'Grape and Vine,' (2) 'Beaded Grape,' (3) 'Queen Victoria,' (4) Ontario 'Maple Leaf' and (5) 'Starflower.' The 'Queen Victoria' does not bear a picture of the Queen, but the decoration is identical with that around the rim of the 'Queen Victoria' plate and on other glassware commemorating the Queen's Jubilee of 1887.*

The pattern on the fifth nappie is regarded by some collectors as distinct from the 'Starflower' because no flowers are shown; others consider it to be merely a variant of the same pattern.

PLATE 38 *Clear glass cup, etched 'Faye, 1887.' Mrs. Daniel Stewart of Woodstock, N.B., formerly Faye Campbell, presented this cup to the authors, stating that she remembered it being blown and etched for her by an itinerant glass-blower at a fair in Woodstock in 1887, when she was five years old.*

PLATES 39 TO 42 *These four bowls or low comports have something in common among themselves as well as with the four Nova Scotian nappies in Plate 36. Whether or not they were made originally in Nova Scotia, Quebec is the province where they are usually found now. The one with the trail-work around the brim (Plate 40) was made in pale green and pale blue as well as colourless glass. The alternate large and small scallops on the bowl in Plate 41 are stoutly maintained by some well-informed Maritimers to be typical Nova Scotian.*

68 PLATE 43 *'Prism and Diamond' comport.*
Here is a true mystery. The base is
unmistakably Lamont 'Pillar.' The finial
on the cover is just as unmistakably N.S.
Glass Co. 'Starflower.' The little ridges
around the circumference of the cover seem
the same as those on the Lamont nappie
(Plate 36). So far as we know no one has
traced the source of the prisms and diamonds.
If it were not for that finial one would be
inclined to say the whole thing was Lamont,
but is it likely that Lamont would adopt
the identical finial used by its competitors
and rivals? Also, would Lamont demean
its magnificent 'Pillar' pattern by
scrambling it with other designs? The
mystery deepens when we look at Plate 44,
where we find a centre that is pure 'Pillar'
surrounded by 'Prism and Diamond.'
So many of the assumed facts are at present
not much more than conjectures that any
theory based upon them may suddenly
collapse with the finding of new evidence,
but for want of a better explanation our
suggestion is that the Diamond Co., having
acquired the moulds of both the Trenton
companies and brought them to Montreal,
scrambled them itself. It may even have
found the 'Pillar' bowls difficult to make
in quantity, as indeed they must have
been, so the less exacting 'Prism and
Diamond' was designed as a substitute.
This would make the date 1899 or later.
In any event quantity was certainly
produced, and many examples are still to
be found. The comports are in several
shapes, some without covers and with
scalloped edges.

PLATE 44 *'Prism and Diamond' cake plate. The diamonds are not flat-sided as in cut glass; in the centre of each is a round 'hobnail,' through or over which there are ridges in the form of an X which extend to the points of the diamond. Observe that the four-pointed star in the middle of the plate is derived from the 'Pillar' pattern: for example see Plate 31.*

70

PLATE 45 *This open comport is obviously a near relative of the 'Prism and Diamond' but here the diamonds are more properly termed squares. Perhaps the pattern might be called 'Bars and Squares.' Each square surrounds a 'hobnail' with an* X *mark, as described above. This may have been a predecessor of 'Prism and Diamond'; the base is plain and the pattern is not quite so frequently encountered.*

PLATE 46 *From left to right, Nova Scotia 'Diamond' goblet; wine-glass and goblet of 'Notched Bull's-eye'; 'Chandelier' tumbler. George MacLaren has authenticated the 'Diamond' as made by one of the companies in Trenton, N.S. The 'Notched Bull's-eye' pattern (so named from the notches above and below the 'eye') was produced by the North American Glass Co., Montreal, one of the successors of the St. Johns companies, from 1885 on. The 'Chandelier' pattern is attributed to a Toronto company. Lee and Metz list it in their books, but do not know its origin.*

PLATE 47 *Maple Leaf patterns. There are at least three easily distinguishable maple leaves in old Canadian glass. The one at the top is the 'Concordia' type, as found on the plate of that name and various other pieces probably made in Montreal in the 1890's (see note to Plate 48). At lower left is the one found on numerous comports, bowls, pitchers and other ware made in Ontario in the early twentieth century. The third, lower right, appears on table sets of cream jug, covered sugar bowl, covered butter dish, and spoon-holder (Plate 51). It too probably originated in Ontario.*

74 PLATE 48 *'Concordia' plate, bearing the crest of the City of Montreal and the city's motto 'Concordia Salus.' This was surely not a mere souvenir to be sold to tourist visitors to Montreal; the crest would mean nothing to them without 'Souvenir of Montreal' emblazoned somewhere. The greater likelihood is that it was made for sale or presentation to Montrealers themselves, in which case it is almost certain to have been a product of the local glass works, i.e., Excelsior, North American, or Diamond. One can hardly imagine either an outside company developing such an idea on its own or a local organization ordering the plate to be made by an outside company. Note the way the maple leaves are drawn, with unrealistically thick, curved and pointed stems. Commemorative plates were a vogue in the 1880's and 90's (e.g., the Queen Victoria plates), and the 'Concordia' was probably made at that time.*

PLATE 49 *Covered butter dish with the 'Concordia' maple leaf, clearly related to the 'Concordia' plate (Plate 48) and probably made in Montreal in the 90's.*

PLATE 50 *'Maple Leaf' plate with the 'Concordia' type of leaf, probably made in Montreal in the 1890's. Due to the easily broken points of the leaves an undamaged specimen of this pattern is rarely found, and is a prize to be treasured.*

PLATE 51 *'Maple Leaf' spoon-holder,
covered sugar bowl, and cream jug, in clear
glass. Sets, including butter dish, are also
found more rarely in green glass and white
and blue 'opal.' There have been claims that
these pieces were made in Nova Scotia, but if
so how can it be explained that the decoration
around the top and bottom of each bowl is
exactly the same as that of the Ontario
pattern? The leaf on the bowl is quite
distinctive, but that on the cover of the
sugar bowl is virtually the same as the
one on the foot of the Ontario comport,
Plate 52. We are led to the conclusion that
if this glass is Nova Scotian, one house or
the other did some very exact copying of
parts of the other's pattern. Ontario
factories did copy several U.S. patterns—
'Nugget,' 'Chandelier,' 'Daisy and X-Band,'
'Daisy and Depressed Button'—but as to
this 'Maple Leaf' pattern the evidence to
date is that it originated in Ontario and
was produced by the Burlington, Sydenham,
and Jefferson companies.*

PLATE 52 *A rare example of Ontario 'Maple Leaf' open comport, the bowl having a waved edge instead of the usual plain round brim. The stippled leaves are sharply pointed and well raised, with narrow stems. Note the shape of the base. Comports in patterns illustrated in the next six plates, 53 to 58, all have bases of identical size and shape, indicating with reasonable certainty that all seven patterns had common or allied origins. These origins are believed to be the Sydenham Co. in Wallaceburg after 1894 and the Jefferson Co. in Toronto after about 1911.*

PLATE 53 *'Nugget' spooner, covered sugar bowl and cream jug; Ontario. This pattern must have been produced in great quantities and within comparatively recent times, judging by the amount to be found now. Gerald Stevens has obtained some information that an earlier version of this pattern, apparently identical with the U.S. 'Shell and Jewel,' was produced in Canada. The older pattern is more attractive and better made, but be careful of what appear to be modern reproductions of the 'Shell and Jewel.'*

PLATE 54 *Covered comport of a pattern that might be called 'Palm and Diamond-point.' The foot is distinctively Ontario in shape, although we have found examples of this pattern from Vancouver to the Maritimes. For some reason, possibly because of a slight excess of manganese in* *the mix when this pattern was being made, the 'Palm and Diamond-point' has a greater tendency than others to take on an amethyst tinge when exposed to long periods of sunlight.*

82

PLATE 55 *A table set of 'Palm and Diamond-point' pattern. A cream pitcher with a cover is unusual, but no doubt this was a useful addition before window-screens became universal!*

PLATE 56 *'Beaded Oval' spooner, sugar bowl, and cream jug. Comports and cake plates in this pattern have the identifying Ontario shape of foot similar to that of the 'Maple Leaf,' 'Palm and Diamondpoint,' and others. The 'Beaded Oval' pattern also appears on various fruit bowls and small dishes.*

PLATE 57 *This is sometimes called the 'Bow Tie' pattern. The base of the comport relates this to other well-known Ontario patterns; see Plate 52. The examples pictured are in clear glass, but the pattern is occasionally found in green.*

84

PLATE 58 *Open comport of a pattern that might be given the name 'Totem' from the curious decoration between the sunbursts. This is another product of Ontario, either Toronto or Wallaceburg.*

PLATE 59 *The 'Beaver' sealer, made in Montreal about 1900. The clear-glass ones are not rare, but the deep-amber ones are exceedingly so. Look in your cellar—you may find a fortune!*

PLATE 60 *Chain drape of clear glass, amber and milk glass, made by a glassblower in the Diamond Flint Glass Co., Ltd., Montreal. Some of these whimsies run to remarkable lengths; one continuous chain in our collection, made by a blower in the Burlington Works about 1885, is over eleven feet long.*

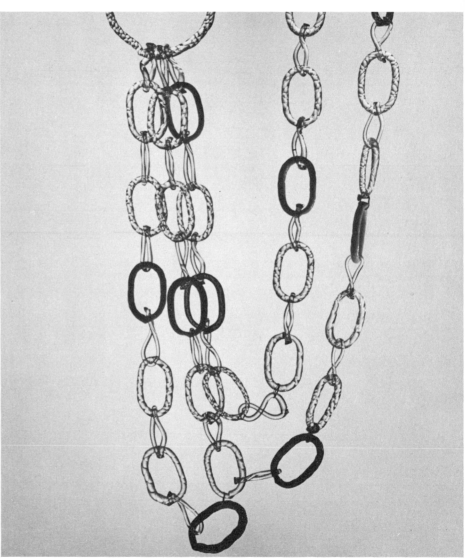

PLATE *61 For no definable reason this has been suspected for a long time of being a Canadian pattern, and it was learned recently that Mrs. J. D. Robinson of Toronto, one of the outstanding authorities on Canadian glass, had traced it to the* Jefferson Glass Co., Toronto. Unless someone discovers another name it might be called 'Crocus.'

PLATE 63 *Thre[...]
'Crocus' pattern [...]
Toronto, 'Canadia[...]on
Glass Works, Ha[...]
the Burlington Co[...]of
others. The 'Drape[...]
an example of it in t[...]*

*Museum authenticated by an accompanying
shard of a large portion of the stem. The
pleated or ribbed parts at the top and bottom
of this stem are sometimes found in other
lamps and may give clues to further
discoveries.*

PLATE 64 *Open comport, 'Daisy and Depressed Button,' made in Burlington Glass Works, Hamilton, in coloured as well as clear glass. Some pieces of this pattern have merely a short glass peg in place of the pedestal, the peg fitting into a hollow in a silver-plated basket stamped with the name of a Toronto company such as Toronto Silver Plate Co. or Acme Silver Co. These two companies were operating in the 80's and into the early part of the twentieth century. The pattern is sharply incised and the button is deeply depressed. The same pattern was made in the U.S. in 1894.*

PLATE 65 *'Rayed Heart' sugar bowl and butter dish; Jefferson Glass Co., Toronto and Sydenham Glass Co., Wallaceburg, twentieth century.*

PLATE 66 *Covered sugar bowl, 'Stippled Swirl and Star'; Jefferson Glass Co., Toronto, and Sydenham Glass Co., Wallaceburg, twentieth century.*

PLATE 67 *'Daisy and* **X***-Band' miniature sugar bowl, full-sized fruit bowl and nappy. This pattern is said to have been made by the Jefferson Glass Co., Toronto, after 1915. The identical pattern was made in the U.S.; if you can distinguish the faint image of a bee in the bottom of the bowl it is not Canadian.*

ENIGMAS AND WILD SURMISES

THE PICTURES to follow are of miscellaneous pieces of glass that may or may not be of Canadian origin; all that the authors can say is that for one reason or another they have 'rung a bell,' had something about them reminiscent of Canadian design, or have been given some authentication short of full proof — although it may be true.

The enthusiastic collector is a pathetically gullible person. He is passionately eager to believe that every goose is a swan, that the proprietor of Joe's Junk Shop is an authority because he is in the 'antique business,' and that the dear old lady's story of the piece having been in the family for generations is utterly reliable, whereas in fact she has forgotten the day in 1910 when she bought it in the Yonge Street Arcade.

So let the reader be warned — don't take it as gospel truth that a piece of glass is early Canadian just because it is pictured here.

Be a little skeptical in all your collecting, but also a little receptive to new ideas. Remember that the Canadian glass-houses turned out thousands of tons of products of great variety. These patterns and designs have not completely disappeared; they must be standing there before us, waiting to be identified.

PLATE 68 *Ruth Webb Lee's* Victorian Glass *calls this 'Diamond Medallion,' and adds that although it is found in New England little is known of its origin. The pattern is plentiful in Canada, and there is an enticing clue in the pedestal of the comport, which is exactly the same as the one found on many pieces of 'Star-flower.' The evidence is tenuous, but we hazard a guess that the Diamond Glass Co. of Montreal made this pattern, achieving a little surreptitious advertising with the diamond in the design.*

PLATE 69 *These two goblets* may *have been made in Hudson, Que. They were among the effects of a very old lady, lifelong resident of Como. She had maintained that they came from one of the local factories, but we doubt this, as they are unlike anything else we have found from that source. The lines around the bowl are moulded into the glass, not ground or etched. The goblets are found occasionally in Quebec and Eastern Ontario, and whether or not they are Hudson, they are probably Canadian.*

96

PLATE 70 *Three pitchers that we strongly suspect to be early Nova Scotian, although we have not yet been able to prove it. The general shape, the shape of the foot, the scalloped edge, the appearance and feel of the non-lead glass, all seem to suggest a* *Canadian origin. Dr. Lorne Pierce had a pitcher the same as the one on the right, as to which he entertained the same suspicions.*

PLATE 71 *Two whimsies, free-blown, of a very strong blue, believed to be Canadian mainly because they came from the collection of a highly respected authority on Canadiana. Unfortunately they cannot be traced farther back. The blue is precisely that of one of the Hudson lamps in Plate 14.*

PLATE 72 *'Chain' pattern sugar bowl,
rumoured among collectors to be Canadian.
R.W. Lee in all her searchings in the
U.S. came across only one example of this
pattern, a small butter dish, but it is
frequently encountered in Canada. Perhaps
the rumour is correct.*

PLATE 73 *Large, very heavy goblet or beer glass made for the Nugget Hotel, Winnipeg. The Nugget Hotel opened in 1899, and closed only recently. The goblet was designed to hold a five-cent beer (26 ounces!). The glass is very clear, but of a steel-blue tinge quite different from glass made in eastern Canada and perhaps indicating sand of a different quality. It is reasonable to guess that the goblet may have been made by the Manitoba Glass Co., which was operating in the early years of the century.*

100

PLATE 74 *Lamp, height 7¼ inches,*
popularly believed to be of Canadian origin,
but so far as we know not yet authenti-
cated. These lamps come in several sizes.

PLATE 75 *Here is a double enigma.
Is there one pattern, or are there two? Ruth
Webb Lee indicates that there are two,
which are sought after in the U.S. but
not well known. She calls one the 'Canadian'
pattern and the other 'Cape Cod,' but her
own illustrations seem to confuse the two.
One gathers that in the example pictured
here she would call the cover 'Cape Cod' and
the bowl 'Canadian,' and in fact the cover
probably did belong originally to something else. However, if there are two
patterns they are so similar that they must
have come from the same source.*

*The next question is, what is that
source? Neither Lee nor Metz can say. Lee
ponders over why a pattern should have
been given the name 'Canadian,' when all
she knows of Canadian glass is a vague
rumour of a factory at Mallorytown, Ont.,
and she ends by saying that the pattern
was probably made in 'America.'*

*Obviously the Mallorytown suggestion
is wrong; figured pressed glass was not
made in those days. But where did the name
'Canadian' come from, and why is it
that although the pattern is apparently
not common in the U.S. one frequently
encounters it in Canadian shops? We can
only throw in the comment that the foot of
the comport resembles some 'Tassel and
Crest' (Plate 25).*

PLATE 76 *This pattern is often found in Canada, does not appear in the U.S. books, and seems to have something Canadian about the shape of the foot and stem. Here is a challenge for someone.*

PLATE 77 *(opposite) Lamp with a simple squirrel pattern in clear glass, the bowl blown into a mould. It is found in Nova Scotia, and well-informed people there insist that it is a product of that province. So far we have found no way of proving it. The pattern is known, although rare, in the U.S., and its source has not been identified.*

PLATE 78 *Wherever one goes in Canada one encounters this pattern. The U.S. writers mention it and Metz calls it 'Aegis,' but R. W. Lee had seen only four examples and concluded that 'probably not much of this design was ever made.' Our guess is that what she saw had been among the thousands of tons of Canadiana pouring into the U.S. from this country. So far we have no clue as to which, if any, Canadian glassworks produced it except that the simple pattern and unsophisticated workmanship indicate an origin not later than the early 80's.*

PLATE 79 *This square 9¾" plate is a true enigma; there are unmistakable maple leaves around the rim and suggestions of fleurs-de-lys and shamrocks in the centre. The crosses in the middle pattern may indicate that the plate was made for religious purposes. This one was found in Quebec, but we have seen another in Barrie, Ont. The workmanship is good and the centre part is very deeply and boldly impressed.*

PLATE 80 *Fragment of slightly green hand-blown window glass, bearing the 'bullion' where the pontil rod was attached. It has been scratched with a diamond 'James Ballard Montreal 1810 May 8th AE 22.' This was from a window of a very old Montreal residence. The glass is undoubtedly of great age, having been made by the ancient 'crown' process of blowing a large bubble of glass, attaching a pontil rod opposite the blowpipe, removing the blowpipe and spinning the punctured bubble on the punty until it opened out into a flat sheet or disc and hardened.*

Unless the scratching on the glass is a hoax, which is unlikely in this case, the pane was in place in 1810 and perhaps earlier. It had probably been imported, but there is always the chance that it came from some unknown local glassworks. One might hope that a record could be found of a James Ballard, born in 1788, possibly on May 8.

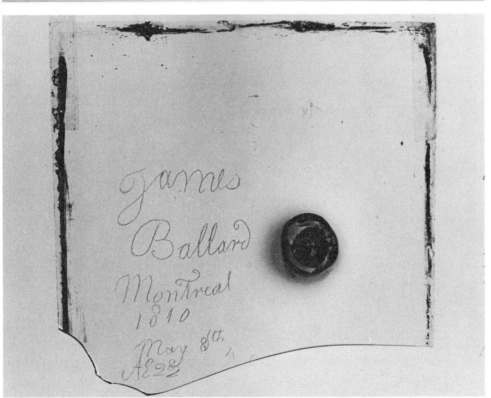

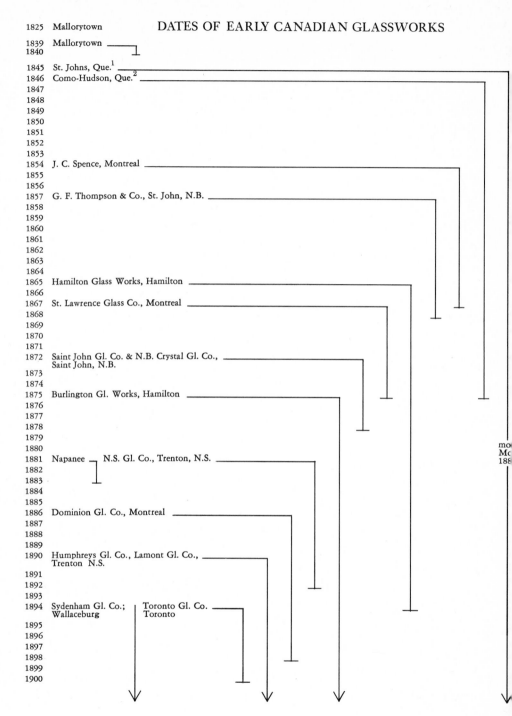

DATES OF EARLY CANADIAN GLASSWORKS

1825 Mallorytown
1839 Mallorytown
1840
1845 St. Johns, Que.[1]
1846 Como-Hudson, Que.[2]
1847
1848
1849
1850
1851
1852
1853
1854 J. C. Spence, Montreal
1855
1856
1857 G. F. Thompson & Co., St. John, N.B.
1858
1859
1860
1861
1862
1863
1864
1865 Hamilton Glass Works, Hamilton
1866
1867 St. Lawrence Glass Co., Montreal
1868
1869
1870
1871
1872 Saint John Gl. Co. & N.B. Crystal Gl. Co.,
     Saint John, N.B.
1873
1874
1875 Burlington Gl. Works, Hamilton
1876
1877
1878
1879
1880
1881 Napanee — N.S. Gl. Co., Trenton, N.S.
1882
1883
1884
1885
1886 Dominion Gl. Co., Montreal
1887
1888
1889
1890 Humphreys Gl. Co., Lamont Gl. Co.,
     Trenton N.S.
1891
1892
1893
1894 Sydenham Gl. Co.; | Toronto Gl. Co.
     Wallaceburg   Toronto
1895
1896
1897
1898
1899
1900

[1] *St. Johns companies were Foster Bros., Excelsior Glass Co., and after move to Montreal, North American Glass Co. and Diamond Glass Co.*

[2] *Como-Hudson companies were Masson & Co., Ottawa Glass Co., Canada Glass Works, British-American Glass Co., Canada Glass Co., Canada Glass Works Co., Ltd.*

III